Contents

Scandinavian Holidays

Lent
It is customary to eat hearty rich foods during the days before the Lenten fast. Shrove Tuesday, the day before the start of Lent is widely celebrated in Scandinavia. The usual fare is a rich meat stew (page 37) and Shrove Tuesday buns (page 108).

Easter
The egg is a symbol of new and eternal life and is an important part of the Easter celebration. Traditional meals vary; pork and lamb are favorites. The Swedes and Norwegians like to include fish in nearly every menu. On Good Friday halibut is served in many Swedish homes.

St Urho's Day

A Finnish invention used to brighten the time around the Ides of March. Each March 16th Finnish-Americans don the green and royal purple and give thanks to the legendary St. Urho for saving the "grape crop" of Finland from the grasshoppers. He drove them from the country with the cry "Grasshopper, grasshopper, go away from here!" Which sounds much better in Finnish: "Heinäsirkka, heinäsirkka, mene täältä hiiteen!"

April First

April Fools' day is celebrated with a passion in Scandinavia. Some years ago, Swedish television pulled the best prank in recent history. A program demonstrated "an invention" that transformed a black-and-white television image into color. How? By stretching a piece of nylon stocking over the screen. Many of the viewing public spent an evening in front of their sets peering in vain for signs of color through ruined stockings.

The Feast of Valborg, April 30th
This is a Swedish celebration of the end of winter. Parties and poems of thanks hail the coming of summer.

May Day
May Day is similar to Labor Day in the United States.

Syttende Mai
May 17 is Norwegian independence day. On January 14, 1814, after four centuries of Danish control, Norway was transferred to Swedish control. In response to the transfer, the Norwegians held elections and chose delegates to a Constituent Assembly which on May 17 declared Norway independent. Sweden sent troops and delayed Norway's independence until 1904. Syttende Mai has become a children's day with hot dogs and ice cream favored as the meal of the day in Norway. Parades that lampoon political leaders have become popular. In America, Stoughton, Wisconsin has an "Ugliest Troll" contest.

Seaman's Day
In late May a day is dedicated to Icelandic sailors.

Ascension Day
The Thursday of the sixth week after Easter brings a religious celebration that has become another celebration of summer.

Whit Sunday—Pentecost
The seventh Sunday after Easter is a religious holiday. Swedes decorate their homes with flowers and branches. It is common for children to be confirmed into the Lutheran faith on Whit Sunday, and Whit Sunday weddings are also popular.

Mother's Day
The last Sunday in May is like a birthday for mothers across Scandinavia.

Sweden's National Day—Flag Day
June 6 is celebrated with parades, speeches and brass bands.

Swedish Birthdays
Every fifth year, particularly at 10, 20, 25, 30, 35, and 40, birthday celebrations begin at 6 A.M. with singing and flag raising. As many as 200 people arrive for the open house and big dinner party. The table is loaded with flowers and gifts.

Iceland's National Day—Flag Day
June 17 is celebrated with parades and street dances.

Midsummer Day and Midsummer Eve
On the morning of Midsummer Eve, June 23rd, Scandinavians decorate their homes, cars, churches and other gathering areas with flowers and leafy branches. That evening bonfires mark the day. Many city dwellers head for the country, where rural festivals and May Pole celebrations are popular.

The Crayfish Premiere and The "Sour Herring" Premiere (Sweden)
The second Wednesday in August is the start of the crayfish fishing season and it takes on a festive air. The week following the opening is filled with parties dedicated to eating the small crustaceans. In the north part of Sweden crayfish do not flourish, so the third Thursday of August became the "Sour Herring" Premiere. Small Baltic herring are salted and set aside to begin a souring process. When the process is under way the fish are hermetically sealed in tins, which are swollen by the time of sale. When a can is opened a pungent aroma fills the room. The fish is served with almond potatoes from the north of Sweden.

Leif Ericson Day
The 9th of October commemorates the Norwegian-born, Icelandic-claimed explorer who landed on the North American mainland in 1000 A.D.

All Saints' Day
The Saturday following the 30th of October is similar to the Memorial Day observed in many communities of the United States. Swedes honor the memory of friends and family members who died in service to their country.

Saint Martin's Day
November 10 traditionally marks the end of autumn's work and the beginning of winter activities. Goose is traditionally served in southern Sweden for this Saint's day.

Iceland's Independence Day
On December 1, 1918 Iceland gained independence from Denmark.

Advent
Advent is four Sundays before Christmas and marks the beginning of Christmas celebrations.

St. Lucia Day (Sweden)

Once thought to be the longest night of the year, an artifact of an early calendar, the 13th of December was the time when man and beast needed extra nourishment. The original holiday was dedicated to St. Lucia of Syracuse, Sicily. Hence each home, community, office, school or club selects a Lucia; in families the eldest daughter portrays Lucia. When morning arrives, the selected Lucia, dressed in a white gown with a crown of candles, carries a tray of coffee, St. Lucia's saffron bread, and cookies to her parents.

Christmas Eve

In Sweden Christmas Eve includes a smörgåsbord and Swedes await the visit of Tomte, the Christmas gnome.

American Danes often celebrate Little Christmas on December 24 with an open house. Upon arrival guests are offered dozens of types of cookies.

The Danish and Norwegian Christmas elf is Nisse, and the Icelandic equivalent is Santa Claus.

Christmas Day
Christmas Day is for church services and family gatherings.

Boxing Day
Starting on the day after Christmas small parties and get-togethers are held until Knut's Day, January 13 or the 20th day after Christmas, a week after Twelfth Night.

New Year's Eve
New Year's Eve celebrations vary from quiet gatherings in front of a television set to large parties and fireworks extending into the wee hours of the morning.

Twelfth Night or Epiphany
January 6 and 7 are celebrated as an extension of Christmas festivities. Cakes, cookies, and candies are served, and the Christmas decorations are torn down.

Thorrablot

According to the old Icelandic calendar the 4th winter month, Thorri, begins on January 21. In pagan times Icelandic people offered sacrifices to their gods. After 1000 A.D., when the country adopted Christianity, this practice was forbidden. Thorri, the ancient god of weather, commanded respect in a country where winter plays a forceful role in the lives of men; a few well-intentioned sacrifices might appease Thorri, although there are no records to determine whether it was an effectual method. One act of sacrifice was to hop around half-naked in the snow early on the first morning of Thorri's month to welcome him home. Also the wife had to treat the husband very well on this day. That must have been a great sacrifice, especially if she began her day by cavorting around in the snow. Thankfully such sacrifices gradually disappeared, but Thorri was not forgotten. Thorri's comeback began in the 19th century and Thorri's time is presently celebrated with dances, parties and songfests. Typical pre-refrigeration Icelandic dishes are served.

Sites Worth Visiting: Swedish

Fort Christiana, State Park, Wilmington, Delaware where the first Swedes and Finns landed on "the rocks" in 1638.

The American Swedish Historical Foundation and Museum, Philadelphia, Pennsylvania.

Gloria Dei (Old Swedes) Church of Philadelphia, Pennsylvania

Holy Trinity (Old Swedes Church) Wilmington, Delaware.

Swedish American Museum, Chicago, Illinois.

Carl Sandburg Birthplace, Galesburg, Illinois.

Carl Sandburg Home, (Connemara) Flat Rock, North Carolina.

Jenny Lind Chapel, Andover, Illinois.

Bishop Hill Colony, Bishop Hill, Illinois.

(continued)

New Sweden Farmstead Museum, Bridgeton, New Jersey.
Stanton, Iowa with a "coffee-pot" water tower.
Mamie Doud Eisenhower Birthplace, Boone, Iowa.
American Swedish Institute, Minneapolis, Minnesota.
Charles A. Lindbergh House, Little Falls, Minnesota.
Gammelgården, Swedish Heritage Museum, Scandia, Minnesota.
Kanebec County Museum, Mora, Minnesota
Lindsborg, Kansas.
Kingsburg, California with a "coffee-pot" water tower.

Sites Worth Visiting: Norwegian

Vesterheim, the Norwegian-American Museum, Decorah, Iowa.
  Permanent collection, outdoor museum complex, pioneer farmstead.
Little Norway, Blue Mounds, Wisconsin. Pioneer homestead and a *stavkirke*
  (Norwegian timber church). Interesting antiques.
Heritage-Hjemkomst Interpretive Center, Moorhead, Minnesota,
  includes a 20th century Viking ship and exhibits.
The Norwegian Pavillion, World Showcase, Epcot Center,
  Walt Disney World, Lake Buena Vista, Florida.
Chapel in the Hills, Rapid City, South Dakota.
  The chapel is a replica of a 12th century Norwegian stave church.

Sites Worth Visiting: Danish

The Danish Windmill and Danish Immigrant Museum site, Elk Horn, Iowa.
A replica of the famed Little Mermaid sculpture that was inspired by a Hans
   Christian Anderson story, Kimballton, Iowa.
Solvang, California. A Danish town with many windmills and attractions, all
   in the north European architectural style. There is a Little Mermaid replica
   gracing a Solvang fountain.

Sites Worth Visiting: Finnish

Suomi College, Hancock, Michigan.
Pioneer Square Museum, Brocket, North Dakota.
Palkie Grist Mill Museum, Esko, Minnesota.
Eli Wirtanen Finnish Farmstead, Markham, Minnesota.

Sites Worth Visiting: Scandinavian

Old World Wisconsin at Eagle, Wisconsin features pioneer farmsteads of various
ethnic groups including Finnish and Norwegian.

Poulsbo, Washington. The third weekend in October thousands come to eat the
annual First Lutheran Church dinner at which almost a ton of lutefisk is
served. (They also serve meatballs.)

Nordic Heritage Museum, Seattle, Washington.

Scandinavian Festivals Across America

Most of the sites listed have special events spring through Christmas. For up-to-date information, contact the Chamber of Commerce in the communites. Cities going all out for their festivals include Elk Horn and Decorah, Iowa; Minneapolis and St. Paul, Minnesota; Bishop Hill, Illinois; Lindsborg, Kansas; Minot, North Dakota; Solvang and Kingsburg, California; Poulsbo, Washington and Astoria, Oregon. Every site listed has special events commemorating Scandinavian heritage, as do most of the colleges founded by Scandinavians.

Menus

Smörgåsbord

Beer & Aquavit
Mushroom Salad
Meatballs
Matjes Herring
Marinated Salmon
Jansson's Temptation
Boiled New Potatoes
Rusk
Potato & Barley Flat Bread
Spritz
Rosettes

Cold Table

Beer & Aquavit
Herbed Danish Blue Cheese Dip &
    Raw Vegetables
Assorted Cheeses & Crackers
Copenhagen Salad
Danish Cucumber Salad
Spiced Meat Roll
Danish Liverpâté
Mustard Herring
Holiday Bread
Icelandic Rolled Cookies

Menus

St. Lucia's Day Breakfast

Egg Coffee
Glögg
St. Lucia's Saffron Bread
Cardamom Horns
Almond Tarts

Christmas Eve Dinner

Glögg
Dip-In-The-Kettle Soup
Swedish Rye Bread
Kräm (fruit pudding)
Assorted Cookies

Menus

Christmas Dinner

Glögg
Herring Salad
Scandinavian Holiday Salad
Christmas Ham with Prunes
Creamed Potatoes
Red Cabbage
Christmas Rice Porridge
Assorted Cookies

New Year's Day Football Viewing Menu

Beer & Aquavit
Herring Pâté
Raw Vegetables
Pea Soup
Icelandic Brown Bread
Assorted Cookies
More Beer & Aquavit

Menus

Midsummer's Eve Dinner

Sima (Finnish Lemon Punch)
Summer Soup
Green Salad
Pastry Covered Salmon with
    Horseradish Sauce
Creamed Kale
Boiled New Potatoes
Lingonberry Torte

Midsummer's Day Lunch

Beer Punch
Cold Buttermilk Soup
Carrot Salad
Hamburger a la Lindström
Herring Salad
Hard Tack
White Potato Bread
Cloudberries with Whipped Cream

Appetizers & Beverages

Herring Pâté

1 12-ounce jar herring in cream
   or wine sauce, drained
1 8-ounce package cream cheese

1/2 cup pitted ripe olives
1/3 cup chopped parsley
1/4 to 1/2 teaspoon curry powder
   juice of 1/2 a lemon

Place all ingredients in a blender and process at the highest speed until smooth.
Place mixture in a crock and chill. Serve on party rye with chopped olives and
hard-cooked egg. Herring Pâté can also be served with raw vegetables.

Herbed Danish Blue Cheese Dip

1/2 cup sour cream
1/3 cup mayonnaise
1 tablespoon lemon juice
1/2 teaspoon tarragon

12/ teaspoon dried dill weed
1 clove garlic minced
2 tablespoons minced green onion
1/4 cup chopped watercress
1/2 cup Danish blue cheese, crumbled

Combine all ingredients in order given. Chill covered at least 2 hours. Serve with fresh vegetables.

Danish Blue Cheese Gâteau

2 cups self-rising flour, sifted
pinch salt

Filling:
6 ounces Danish blue cheese,
    mashed
1/2 cup whipping cream,
    whipped, divided

6 tablespoons butter, softened
2 tablespoons mayonnaise
4 to 5 tablespoons milk

1/4 cup chopped celery
pepper to taste
1 medium-sized tomato, thinly sliced
2 ounces cream cheese, softened
celery leaves for garnish

(continued)

Danish Blue Cheese Gâteau *(continued)*

Combine the flour and salt. Cut the butter into the flour. Add the mayonnaise and enough milk to make a soft dough. Knead and divide dough in half. Roll out first half and cut into an 8-inch circle; place on a greased baking sheet. Roll out second half; place on another greased baking sheet and cut into 8 wedges. Bake at 400° for 15 minutes. Cool on baking sheets.

Filling: Combine the blue cheese with two-thirds of the whipped cream, celery, and pepper; mix well. Place the 8-inch pastry circle on a plate and arrange all but 4 of the tomato slices over it. Spread the blue cheese mixture over tomato slices. Place the 8 triangles over the cheese. Combine the remaining whipped cream and cream cheese. Place the cream cheese mixture into a piping bag and pipe a rosette on top of each triangle. Decorate with celery leaves and reserved tomato slices.

Egg Coffee
Sweden

5 cups cold water
6 rounded teaspoons coffee

1 1/2 teaspoons egg, slightly beaten
1 teaspoon cold water
2 tablespoons cold water

Bring 5 cups of water to a boil. Mix coffee, egg, and 1 teaspoon cold water. Add to boiling water. Let simmer 3 to 4 minutes. Pour 2 tablespoons cold water into coffee pot spout to settle coffee grounds. Makes 5 cups.

Eggnog

8 egg yolks
4 tablespoons confectioners' sugar

4 cups orange juice
1 cup brandy

Beat together egg yolks and sugar. Add orange juice and brandy. Serves 4.

Beer Punch

12 ounces pale ale, cold
12 ounces light-colored beer, cold

12 ounces dark beer, cold
1/3 cup aquavit, ice cold

Gradually pour all very cold ingredients, in order given, into a chilled pitcher. Gently stir. Serve in mugs. Serves 6.

Sima
Finland

2 lemons
4 quarts water
2 1/2 cups brown sugar, packed
1 envelope active dry yeast

1/4 teaspoon ground ginger
12 ounces light-colored beer, if desired
2 tablespoons sugar, divided
1 tablespoon raisins, divided

Scrape all the yellow lemon zest from the lemons; set aside. Peel and discard the white peel. Slice the lemons very thin. Bring water to a boil and dissolve brown sugar in water. Add lemon zest and slices. Remove from heat and cool. Pour into a large nonmetal container. Stir in yeast, ginger, and beer. Cover and set aside overnight or until little bubbles form. Sterilize pint or quart bottles or a gallon bottle. Scald lids, caps or corks. Add sugar and a few raisins into each bottle. Strain liquid into bottles. Attach caps, lids or corks and set aside until raisins rise to the top, about 8 hours to 2 days. Serve cold.

Scandinavian Beers & Schnapps

Danish Beers: Albani, Carlsberg, Thor, Ceres, Faxe, Neptune, and Tuborg.

Finnish Beer: Koff.

Icelandic Beer: Polar.

Swedish Beers: Pripps and Spendrup's.

Norwegian Beers: Mack, Frydenlund, Aass, Ringnes, and Hansa.

Schnapps: Aquavit is a caraway liquor.

May Pole

Glögg

4 cups of claret or port wine
2 cups dark rum
4 cups brandy, divided
4 cardamom seeds, peeled
3 cinnamon sticks

10 whole cloves
peel of 1/2 lemon, cut into strips
peel of 1/2 orange, cut into strips
1/2 cup blanched almonds
1/2 cup dark raisins
1 cup sugar cubes

Bring wine, rum and 3 cups of brandy to a boil. Tie all spices in a cheesecloth bag. Add bag, almonds, and raisins to hot liquid. Reduce heat. Simmer about 10 minutes. Remove from heat. Place the sugar in a large sieve. With sieve over a saucepan pour some of the hot liquid over the sugar cubes. Set fire to the cubes and continue to spoon the flaming cubes with liquid until they are dissolved. Cool 30 minutes. Add remaining brandy. Refrigerate for a few days and serve hot, garnished with additional raisins and almonds.

Soups & Salads

Norwegian Stew

Serve on May 17, Norway's independence day.

1 1/2 cups diced beef
1/2 cup diced fresh pork
1 1/2 cups cooked, diced corned beef

4 cups diced raw potatoes
1 onion, diced
1/2 teaspoon pepper

Cover meats with water and boil slowly for 1 to 2 hours. Add the remaining ingredients and cook until tender.

Danish Stew

1 2/3 pounds lean beef or veal
5 large onions, chopped
3/4 cup butter
12 whole peppercorns

2 bay leaves
3 pounds potatoes, peeled and diced
6 teaspoons butter, shaped into balls
chopped chives

Sauté meat and onion in 3/4 cup butter until soft. Add boiling water to cover meat and onion, add peppercorns and bay leaves. Simmer for about 20 minutes. Add potatoes. Cook until the potatoes have blended with the meat broth, giving the appearance of a very thick soup. Remove from heat. Place in small dishes, garnish with balls of butter on each and serve with chopped chives on the side. Serves 6.

Yoghurt Soup
Icelandic

1 cup milk
2 cups plain yoghurt
1 small cucumber, finely diced
15 radishes, sliced
2 tablespoons chopped chives

1 tablespoon fresh chopped dill or
   1 teaspoon dried dill
1 1/2 teaspoons fresh chopped tarragon
   or 1/2 teaspoon dried tarragon
pinch of dried mint
salt and white pepper to taste

Combine the milk and yoghurt. Stir in all remaining ingredients. Chill. Serve very cold. Serve 6.

Summer Soup

3 small carrots, chopped
1 cup green peas, fresh or frozen
1/4 head cauliflower,
    cut into flowerets
2 cups water
1 1/2 teaspoons salt

4 ounces fresh spinach, chopped
2 cups milk, divided
1 tablespoon flour
1 egg yolk
3 tablespoons whipping cream
3 tablespoons chopped parsley

Combine carrots, peas, cauliflower, water, and salt. Cook until almost tender; add spinach, cook about 5 minutes. Remove vegetables with a slotted spoon, set aside. Mix 1 tablespoon milk with flour. Add remaining milk to vegetable broth. Add flour mixture to broth. Beat yolk and cream together. Add yolk mixture, vegetables, and chopped parsley to broth. Serve warm. Serves 4.

Finnish Beer Cheese Soup

2 cups milk
2 tablespoons flour
1 tablespoon sugar
salt to taste

1/2 cup Finnish-style beer
1/2 cup beef broth
1 tablespoon dark corn syrup
1/4 teaspoon ground ginger
2 cups diced Swiss cheese

In a saucepan, combine milk, flour, sugar, and salt. Heat to a boil, stirring. Cook, stirring until thickened. Remove from heat. In another saucepan, combine beer, broth, corn syrup, and ginger. Heat to boiling, stirring constantly. Stir into thickened milk mixture. Return to heat and heat to boiling. Place cheese in bottom of soup bowls. Ladle soup into bowls and serve immediately. Serves 6.

Kale Soup
Danish

ham shank or soup bone
1 medium-sized onion, chopped

3/4 cup oatmeal
10 to 12 curly kale leaves
ham, diced, to taste

Cover shank or bone with water and cook 1 to 2 hours to make stock. Remove shank and refrigerate broth overnight. Skim off fat. Add onion and oatmeal to stock and heat. Add kale and cook slowly until kale is tender. Add ham if desired. Serves 4.

Dip-in-the-Kettle Soup
Swedish

6 cups ham or roast beef broth
salt and pepper to taste

Swedish Rye Bread, recipe on page 103
3 tablespoons butter
1/2 lemon, sliced

Heat broth and season to taste. Toast and butter slices of bread. To serve, place pieces of bread into individual serving dishes and pour broth over bread and garnish with lemon slices. Serve with additional bread. Serves 6.

St. Urho's Day Fish Stew
Finnish

6 large potatoes, peeled and cut
    into chunks
1 large onion, diced
2 teaspoons salt
5 whole allspice
6 cups water

3 pounds cleaned fresh water fish
    (trout, walleye, or whitefish)
2 cups cream
2 tablespoons butter
fresh or dried dill to taste

In a large kettle, place potatoes, onion, salt, allspice, and water. Cover and bring to a boil. Reduce heat and simmer for 15 to 20 minutes or until potatoes are tender. Cut fish into bite-sized chunks. Add to potato mixture and simmer covered for 15 more minutes. Stew should not boil. Cook fish until it flakes, no longer. Stir in cream, butter, and dill weed. Serve hot. Serves 6.

Pea Soup

Swedes are noted for Thursday night pea soup dinners.

2 quarts water
2 cups green split peas
1 stalk celery, chopped
dash cayenne pepper

1 large carrot, diced
1 onion, chopped
1/2 teaspoon thyme
1 bay leaf, ground
salt and pepper to taste

Place all ingredients in a large kettle. Cover and bring to a boil. Boil for 20 minutes. Reduce heat and simmer until peas are tender. Press through a fine sieve and reheat. Serves 6 to 8.

Fruit Sago Soup
Danish

8 cups water
1/2 cup sago or 1/3 cup Minute
   Tapioca
1 stick cinnamon

1 cup prunes
1/2 cup fruit juice (peach or pear)
1/2 cup sugar

Bring water to a boil; add sago, cinnamon stick, prunes, and raisins. Simmer until sago is clear. Add juice and sugar. More juice or sugar may be added to taste. Serves 8.

Rum Soup
Danish

2 egg yolks, beaten
1/4 cup sugar

1 tablespoon flour
2 quarts milk, scalded
1/2 cup rum

Beat together yolks, sugar, and flour. Place in a serving bowl and pour the hot milk slowly over the mixture. Stir in the rum. Serve with zwieback.

Cold Buttermilk Soup
Danish

3 ounces sugar
2 egg yolks
lemon juice to taste

1 quart buttermilk, chilled
1 cup heavy cream, whipped
1 1/2 ounces blanched almonds, split
strawberry jam

Beat the sugar and egg yolks together until the mixture becomes light. Add lemon juice. Gradually add buttermilk. Serve this soup very cold, garnished with whipped cream, almonds, and a little strawberry jam. Serves 6.

Mushroom Salad

1 pound fresh mushrooms, whole
2 tablespoons finely minced onion
2 tablespoons fresh lemon juice
1 tablespoon sugar
1/2 teaspoon freshly ground pepper

1/2 cup whipping cream
1/4 cup sour cream
1 teaspoon salt
1/8 teaspoon dry mustard
fresh lettuce for garnish, optional

Combine mushrooms, onion, lemon juice, sugar, and pepper; cover. Refrigerate 30 minutes to 4 hours. Whip cream until thick, fold in sour cream, salt, and mustard. Stir into mushroom mixture. Pour into a serving bowl, lined with lettuce if desired. Serves 8.

Scandinavian Holiday Salad

1 quart cranberries
1 1/2 cups sugar
1 1/2 cups crushed graham crackers

1/2 teaspoon salt
pinch cinnamon
1 1/2 cups whipping cream, whipped

Cook cranberries until soft. Remove and reserve a few whole cranberries for decoration. Add sugar to cranberries; mix well. Cool and refrigerate. Combine crackers, salt, and cinnamon. In a clear glass bowl, alternate layers of cranberry mixture, then cracker mixture, and then whipped cream. Repeat and end with whipped cream. Garnish with reserved cranberries. Serves 10 to 15.

Danish Cucumber Salad

2 8-inch cucumbers
1 cup water, heated
1 cup vinegar

1/4 teaspoon white pepper
salt to taste
1 cup sugar

Slice cucumbers into paper-thin slices. Combine remaining ingredients and stir until sugar dissolves. Stir in cucumbers. Refrigerate at least 5 hours or overnight. Drain and serve. Serves 8.

Carrot Salad

This is a favorite at Lutheran Church suppers.

1 10 1/2-ounce can tomato soup
1 cup sugar
1/4 cup vegetable oil
1/4 cup vinegar
1 teaspoon dry mustard

1 teaspoon Worcestershire sauce
1/2 teaspoon salt
2 pounds carrots, peeled and sliced
1 medium-sized onion, diced
1 green pepper, chopped
1/2 cup chopped celery

Combine soup, sugar, oil, vinegar, mustard, Worcestershire, and salt. Cook for 5 minutes and cool. Cook carrots until tender, and drain. Add onion, green pepper, and celery. Pour sauce over vegetables and marinate overnight.

Copenhagen Salad

6 ounces Danablu (blue cheese)
1/2 pound black grapes, halved
    seeded

4 ounces shelled walnuts, halved
1 11-ounce can mandarin oranges
    white wine

Cube cheese. Add grapes, walnuts, and mandarin oranges. Just before serving
sprinkle with wine.

Meats, Poultry & Fish

53

Spiced Meat Roll

1 flank of beef or lamb
1/2 teaspoon ground allspice
2 tablespoons salt

1/2 teaspoon saltpeter
1 teaspoon pepper
1 onion, chopped
3 or 4 thin slices of pork

Brine:
2 1/2 quarts boiling water

2 cups salt
1/2 teaspoon saltpeter

Flatten meat and sprinkle with spices. Spread with onion and pork. Roll meat tightly like a jellyroll and sew ends and sides. Place in brine for 10 days. After 10 days remove meat from brine and wind with cord. Place in boiling water, reduce heat and cook for 2 hours or until tender. Remove from water and press between two flat surfaces until cold. Slice thinly and serve on bread.

Brine: Combine all ingredients.

Norwegian Meatballs

2 pounds ground beef
1 tablespoon potato flour
1/2 teaspoon nutmeg
2 teaspoons salt
1 tablespoon flour

1 egg
1/2 cup milk
1/2 teaspoon pepper
1/2 teaspoon ginger
1 medium-sized onion, minced

Gravy:
2 tablespoons flour

1 cup milk
dash nutmeg
salt and pepper

Mix all ingredients well and shape into balls. Brown the balls all around in a frying pan. Remove balls from pan and place on a serving platter.

Gravy: Sprinkle drippings from pan with flour and stir. Gradually add milk and stir until smooth. Season to taste.

Grandmother's Swedish Meatballs
Mrs. Dora Benander Koch

Meatballs:
2 pounds ground lean beef
1/2 cup oatmeal
1 egg

2 tablespoons finely minced onion
dash Worcestershire sauce
1/2 teaspoon nutmeg
4 cups cooked rice

Gravy:
1 tablespoon flour

1/2 cup beer
dash nutmeg

Meatballs: Combine all ingredients except rice; mix well. Shape into balls and brown all around in a skillet. Remove balls from pan.

Gravy: Add flour to meatball drippings; stir until smooth. Add beer and nutmeg. If too thick, add more beer; if too thin, add more flour. Stir meatballs into gravy. Serve hot over steaming hot rice.

Hamburger a la Lindström

1 pound lean ground beef
2 egg yolks
1/2 cup juice from pickled beets
1/3 cup heavy cream
salt and pepper to taste

butter
5 tablespoons finely minced onion
3 tablespoons finely chopped capers
1/2 cup finely chopped pickled beets,
    drained

Combine ground beef, egg yolks, juice from the pickled beets, cream, salt, and pepper. Sauté onion in butter until soft. Add onion, capers, and pickled beets to ground beef mixture. Shape into hamburger patties. Cook in a frying pan with butter or on an outdoor grill, 3 to 4 minutes on each side, until they are browned on the outside and rosy in the center.

Traditional Icelandic Sunday Roast

Embassy of Iceland, Washington, D.C.

1 leg of lamb	butter
salt and pepper	stock or hot water
	flour

Wipe lamb with a warm damp cloth. Rub salt and pepper into the meat. Top the roast with a few dots of butter. Place roast into a greased roaster. Bake at 450° for 15 to 20 minutes. Reduce temperature to 350°. Pour stock or water into the roaster and cook for 15 minutes per pound, basting occasionally. When meat is done, skim the excess fat from the drippings and pour the drippings into a saucepan. Add enough flour to the drippings to make a smooth gravy.

Danish Liver Pâté

1 1/2 pounds pig liver
1/2 pound bacon
1/2 medium-sized onion
1 tablespoon chopped anchovies
1 teaspoon salt
1/2 teaspoon pepper

1/2 teaspoon ground cloves
1/2 teaspoon ground allspice
2 tablespoons butter
1/4 cup flour
1 cup milk
1 egg, beaten

Grind liver, bacon, and onion together twice. Add anchovies and all seasonings; blend well. Melt the butter and stir in the flour until smooth. Gradually add milk. Stirring constantly, bring to a boil and cook for 2 to 3 minutes. Add milk mixture to liver mixture. Add egg and beat well. Place mixture into a loaf pan and cover with foil. Place the loaf pan into a 9x13-inch baking dish. Add 1 inch of water to the baking dish. Bake at 325° for 1 to 1 1/2 hours. Cool completely before removing from pan.

Christmas Ham with Prunes

1 fresh ham, 6 to 8 pounds
20 pitted prunes, coarsely chopped
1 cup minced onion
1 1/2 cups pared, chopped apple
1/4 cup applesauce

1 10 1/2-ounce can beef consommé
1 cup currant jelly
1/2 cup orange juice
1/3 cup port wine
1/2 teaspoon salt

Have butcher remove center bone from a fresh ham and cut a deep pocket in the cavity. Combine prunes, onion, apple, and applesauce. Stuff ham with apple mixture, overlap and secure ends. Score the fat side of the ham and place fat side up in a shallow baking dish. Pour consommé over ham. Roast at 325° for 30 to 35 minutes per pound, basting often. Transfer ham to a serving platter and keep warm. Remove and discard fat from pan juices. Bring pan juices to a boil and cook for 5 minutes. Add remaining ingredients and simmer for 10 to 15 minutes. Serve gravy with ham.

Apple-Stuffed Pork Loin

1 pork loin roast, 4 to 6 pounds,
  boneless
1 green apple, peeled, cored,
  and sliced

10 pitted prunes, halved
1 tablespoon salt, divided
1 teaspoon freshly ground black
  pepper, divided
3 cups chicken or beef broth, or beer

Lay meat on a flat surface, fat-side down. Arrange apple slices and prunes over surface of roast. Sprinkle with 1 teaspoon salt and 1/2 teaspoon pepper. Tightly roll the roast, enclosing the filling. Tie roast in at least 3 places. Rub outside of roast with remaining salt and pepper. Place in a deep roasting pan. Bake 2 1/2 to 3 hours or until meat is tender. Baste every 30 minutes with about 1/2 cup of broth or beer. Remove meat to a serving platter and keep warm. Strain pan juices into a saucepan and cook until the sauce is reduced to about 1 cup of glaze. Serve roast with glaze. Serves 8.

Roast Duck

1 5- to 7-pound duck
salt

1/2 pound prunes, soaked and pitted
3 tart apples, peeled, halved, and
cored

Wash, clean and dry duck. Rub inside with salt. Stuff with prunes and apples.
Sprinkle duck with salt and place in an ungreased roasting pan, breast side up.
Roast uncovered at 325° for 45 minutes per pound. Do not prick skin with fork.
Remove excess fat from pan during roasting.

Roast Goose

1 10-pound goose
salt and pepper
1 cup soaked, pitted prunes

1 1/2 cups peeled, cored and sliced apples
4 cups boiling water
flour

Season the goose inside and out with salt and pepper. Stuff with prunes and apples. Place in a large pan and brown the goose on all sides in a hot oven. Add 4 cups boiling water and baste. Roast for 3 hours at 325°. For crisp skin, pour 2 tablespoons of water over the goose and let brown additional 15 minutes. Skim fat from drippings and add flour to thicken for gravy.

Norwegian Chicken & Gjetost Sauce

1 chicken, 3 pounds
salt and white pepper to taste
2 tablespoons butter
1 cup chicken broth

1/2 cup cooking sherry
1/3 cup fresh chopped parsley
1/2 cup heavy cream
1 cup shredded gjetost cheese*
parsley for garnish

Cut chicken into serving-sized pieces and remove skin. Rub chicken with salt and pepper. Brown chicken in butter on all sides. Add broth and sherry to browned chicken. Reduce heat, cover and simmer for 45 minutes, until chicken is tender. Remove chicken to a serving platter and keep warm. Add parsley and cream to drippings. Bring to a simmer, stirring constantly, and cook until sauce is reduced to about 1 cup. Stir in cheese and cook just until it is melted. Pour sauce over chicken and serve garnished with parsley. Serves 4.
*Norwegian goat cheese found in specialty cheese shops.

Matjes Herring

Matjes herring is the most important dish on the Swedish Smörgåsbord.

1 7-ounce can matjes herring*
4 tablespoons chopped chives
3/4 cup sour cream

1 medium-sized red onion, sliced in rings
bunch of fresh dill
1 pound small new potatoes, boiled

Cut herring fillets on the diagonal into 1-inch pieces. Arrange on serving platter. Either combine the chives and sour cream or place in serving dishes separately. Garnish fish with onion rings and dill. Serve with hot potatoes.
*Matjes herring may be purchased in Scandinavian stores and specialty meat markets.

Mustard Herring

3 marinated herring or red herring
2 tablespoons dry mustard
2 tablespoons sugar
dash salt

dash white pepper
1 tablespoon vinegar
2 cups whipping cream, whipped
dill weed

Cut up herring. Arrange on platter. Mix mustard, sugar, salt, pepper, and vinegar. Fold into whipped cream. Place a spoonful on each piece of herring. Garnish with dill.

Herring Salad

3/4 cup chopped pickled herring
1 cup cooked cubed potatoes
1 medium-sized onion, minced
2 hard-cooked eggs, chopped

2/3 cup cooked chopped beets
3 medium-sized dill pickles, chopped
3 tablespoons vinegar
3 ounces cream cheese, softened

Combine herring, potatoes, onion, eggs, beets, and pickles. Beat cream cheese and vinegar together until smooth. Add to herring mixture; blend well.

Fish Mousse

1 1/2 pounds cod fillets
2 teaspoons salt
1/4 teaspoon ground white pepper
dash nutmeg
1 1/2 tablespoons cornstarch

1 1/3 cups milk
1 1/2 cups whipping cream
1 tablespoon butter
1/4 cup soft bread crumbs
chopped fresh parsley

Cut fish lengthwise into strips. Put fish through grinder 3 times. Combine fish purée, salt, pepper, nutmeg, and cornstarch; beat at high speed for 10 minutes. Beat 20 minutes longer, gradually adding milk and whipping cream. Butter a 10-cup ring mold or fancy tube mold and coat with bread crumbs. Butter a 12-inch square of waxed paper. Spoon fish mixture into mold; cover with buttered waxed paper. Place mold into a 9x13-inch pan and pour 1 inch of boiling water into the pan, around the mold. Bake at 375° for 45 minutes or until mixture pulls away from side of pan. Invert mold on a serving dish and garnish with parsley.

Danish New Year's Eve Cod and Mustard Gravy

1 3-pound cod, cleaned
1/4 cup salt, divided

2 tablespoons vinegar
1 quart water

Gravy:
4 tablespoons butter
4 tablespoons flour

1 1/2 cups water from boiling cod
1 1/2 cups milk
1 1/2 tablespoons Dijon mustard
salt to taste

Cut cod into steaks about 1 1/2 inch thick. Sprinkle steaks with 1/2 the salt; set aside for 15 minutes. Rinse steaks. Combine remaining salt, vinegar, and water in a pan; bring mixture to a boil. Add fish, cover, and bring to a boil. Turn off heat and let stand, covered, for 10 minutes. Drain fish on absorbent paper and serve with gravy. Serves 6.

Gravy: In a saucepan, melt butter. Stir in flour until smooth. Gradually add fish water and milk. Cook until thickened. Stir in mustard and salt.

Lutefisk

2 pounds lutefisk   1/2 pound butter, melted

Rinse fish thoroughly in cold water. Cut into serving-size pieces. Wrap fish in
cheesecloth and place in cool salted water. Bring water to a boil. Cook for 10
minutes or until tender and translucent. Remove and serve with generous
amounts of melted butter. Serves 4.

Pastry-Covered Salmon with Horseradish Sauce

2 pounds salmon fillet
6 tablespoons butter, divided
1 tablespoon lemon juice
1/2 teaspoon salt
2 tablespoons fresh minced parsley
3 tablespoons fresh chopped dill

salt and pepper to taste
1 1/2 cups cooked rice
3 hard-cooked eggs, sliced
1 egg, beaten
melted butter
1 lemon, cut into wedges, garnish

Pastry:
1 cup butter

2 cups flour
2 cups cottage cheese
1 to 2 tablespoons ice water

Horseradish Sauce:
1/2 cup heavy cream, whipped
1 cup mayonnaise

3 tablespoons freshly grated
   horseradish root

(continued)

Pastry-Covered Salmon with Horseradish Sauce   *(continued)*

Sauté salmon fillet in 2 tablespoons butter for 2 1/2 minutes on each side. Sprinkle with lemon juice and salt. Trim cooked fish so that it is shaped like fish, 15 inches long. Set aside. Combine salmon trimmings, parsley, dill, salt, and pepper. Refrigerate at least 20 minutes.

Pastry: Cut butter into flour until the mixture resembles corn meal. Add cottage cheese to form a crumbly dough, adding water a few drops at a time so that the dough will form a ball. Chill for 30 minutes.

To Assemble: Divide dough in half. Roll out half the dough into an 18x8-inch oval. Shape 1 end to resemble a fish tail, at least 6 inches wide. Place on a greased baking sheet. Spread parsley mixture over pastry. Melt butter and drizzle over parsley mixture. Top with hard-cooked eggs. Place salmon fillet over eggs.

(continued)

Roll out remaining half of dough to a 20x10-inch oval. Moisten edges of bottom crust with water and place top crust over. Press to seal. Trim the top crust into the shape of a fish, using pastry scraps to represent fins, gills, and eye. Brush pastry with beaten egg. Using the tips of scissors blades, cut marks in top crust to resemble scales. These holes will also serve as vents during baking. Bake at 375° for 35 minutes or until crust is lightly golden. Serve with melted butter, lemon wedges, and horseradish sauce. Serves 8.

Sauce: Fold mayonnaise and horseradish into whipped cream until blended. Refrigerate 15 to 30 minutes.

Marinated Salmon

3-pound piece of salmon, scaled
2 teaspoons vegetable oil
4 tablespoons sugar

3 teaspoons freshly ground pepper
4 tablespoons salt
1 large bunch fresh dill, divided

Cut the salmon down the center and remove the backbone and any small bones. Moisten with oil and rub with sugar, pepper, and salt. Spread about 1/3 the dill in the bottom of a jellyroll pan. Place 1/2 the salmon on dill skin-side down. Cover with the second 1/3 of the dill. Place the remaining salmon skin-side up on this layer. Sprinkle with remaining dill. Place a pan with several full cans or weights on top of the salmon and refrigerate for about 3 days. Scrape off dill and seasonings. Slice diagonally into thin slices. Serve garnished with lemon wedges.

Crayfish
Swedish

large bunch fresh dill
2 1/2 quarts water

1/3 cup plus 1 tablespoon coarse salt
1 lump sugar
2 pounds live crayfish

Combine dill, water, salt, and sugar in a large pot. Cover and bring to a boil. Check the crayfish to see that they are all alive. Place crayfish into boiling water and cover. Bring to a boil and cook 7 minutes from the time the water starts boiling. Let crayfish cool in cooking water. Place in refrigerator overnight while still in the cooking water. To serve, drain and arrange crayfish on a serving platter; garnish with additional fresh dill.

Vegetables & Side Dishes

Creamed Kale	83
Creamed Potatoes	81
Jansson's Temptation	77
Pickled Beets	80
Potato Cakes	82
Red Cabbage	79
Swedish Brown Beans	84
Sweet-Sour Cabbage	78

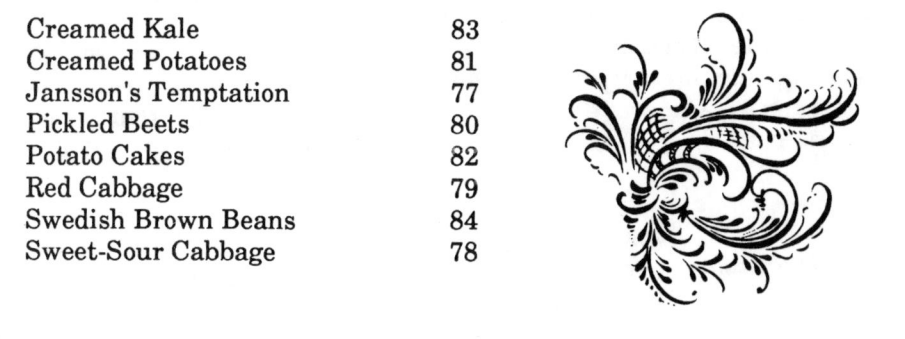

Jansson's Temptation
Swedish

2 large onions, sliced
20 anchovy fillets
6 medium-sized potatoes, pared and
   cut into thin strips

1 to 1 1/2 cups cream
1 tablespoon dried bread crumbs
2 tablespoons butter, optional

Layer onions and anchovy fillets in the bottom of a 9x13-inch baking dish. Cover with potatoes and cover entire mixture with cream. Sprinkle with bread crumbs and dot with butter. Bake at 425° for 45 to 50 minutes.

Sweet-Sour Cabbage
Norwegian

1 head cabbage, finely shredded
1 teaspoon salt
2 tablespoons sugar

1/2 cup water
1/4 cup vinegar
2 tablespoons caraway seed

Combine all ingredients. Bring to a boil and let simmer for 2 to 3 hours. Very good with pork roast.

Red Cabbage

1 3-pound head cabbage
2 tablespoons vinegar
1/4 cup butter

1/4 cup sugar
1 teaspoon salt
1/2 cup red currant jelly
1 medium-sized apple, cored and diced

Shred cabbage and sprinkle with vinegar to keep from darkening. Melt butter, stir in sugar and salt. Add cabbage and cook for 15 minutes. Add remaining ingredients and let simmer for 1 hour. Serve hot. Serves 8.

79

Pickled Beets

8 beets
1 cup sugar

2 cups vinegar
1 cup water
1-inch piece horseradish, divided

Cook beets until tender, about 2 hours. Peel and slice beets. Combine sugar, vinegar, and water, stirring until sugar is dissolved. Place beets in 2 to 4 sterile pint jars and pour vinegar mixture over them. Divide horseradish among the jars, one piece in each. Let stand for 24 hours before serving.

Creamed Potatoes
Swedish

10 medium-sized potatoes peeled and diced

2 tablespoons butter

1 1/2 cups 1/2-and-1/2 cream

1/2 tablespoon salt

1/3 cup finely chopped dill, parsley, chives or leeks—any one or a mixture

Sauté potatoes in butter. Add cream and salt. Cook, covered, over low heat for about 15 to 20 minutes. Add remaining ingredient(s). Serves 4.

Potato Cakes

1/4 pound bacon
4 large potatoes, pared, cooked,
    and mashed
1 tablespoon milk

1 egg, slightly beaten
1/2 teaspoon allspice
1/2 teaspoon salt
1 small onion, finely minced

Cook bacon crisp; drain on absorbent paper, reserving drippings. Crumble bacon into potatoes. Add milk, egg, allspice, salt, and onion. Beat until smooth. Shape into patties and fry in the reserved bacon grease. Serve hot. Serves 4.

Creamed Kale

2 tablespoons butter
2 tablespoons flour

1 cup milk
2 cups finely chopped kale
salt and pepper

Melt butter; add flour and stir until smooth. When mixture gets bubbly, gradually add milk. Cook 5 minutes. Add kale and simmer for 25 to 30 minutes. Season to taste.

Swedish Brown Beans

2 cups beans
5 cups water
1 tablespoon flour

4 tablespoons vinegar
4 tablespoons light molasses
salt to taste

Wash beans; drain. Cook beans in 5 cups water for 3 to 4 hours or until the beans are tender. Add more hot water as needed. Dissolve flour in a little water and add to beans. Add remaining ingredients; cook a few more minutes and serve hot. Serves 6.

Pancakes, Porridges, Puddings, & Pastries

Lefse
Norwegian

5 well-packed cups of cooked,
   riced potatoes
1/2 cup margarine

3 tablespoons powdered sugar
2 cups flour
1 teaspoon salt

Add margarine to potatoes while they are still warm. Cool to room temperature. Add powdered sugar, flour, and salt. Knead well and then roll into a log. Cut and measure into 1/3 cup portions, make a round ball of each. On a floured lefsa "board"* press each dough ball down and then, using a pastry sleeve and rolling pin, roll into 14-inch circles to fit a lefsa griddle*. The secret to making lefse is the use of a lefsa stick*. For the last roll across the dough use a grooved lefsa rolling pin, which marks the dough and makes it thinner. Grill dough on a lefsa griddle for about 1 to 2 minutes on each side. Fold each lefsa in half or quarters. Cool between towels and store in plastic bags.
*Found in specialty and culinary shops.

Danish Pancakes

4 eggs
1/3 cup sugar
1/2 teaspoon salt
6 tablespoons butter, melted

grated peel of 1 lemon
2 cups flour
1 1/2 cups milk
1/2 cup beer
butter for frying

Beat together eggs, sugar, salt, and melted butter. Combine lemon peel and flour. Add flour mixture and milk and beer alternately to egg mixture. Mix well; refrigerate for 1 hour. Heat a frying pan and add some butter. Pour enough batter to create a thin layer on the bottom of the frying pan. Shake the pan while frying to prevent sticking. When edges brown, flip the pancake and brown the other side. Repeat with remaining batter. Serve pancakes filled with stewed apples, jam, chopped almonds or custard cream. Serves 6.

Swedish Pancakes

Glen & Virginia Arnold
The Swedish Mill, Kingsburg, California

2 egg yolks
4 eggs
2 1/4 cups milk

1/4 cup sugar
1 1/2 cups flour
1/2 cup butter, melted

Mix all ingredients together. Set aside for at least 1/2 hour, up to overnight. On a hot griddle spread about 1/4 cup of batter out thinly. Grill on both sides until golden brown. Repeat with remaining batter. Serve with lingonberries, jam or syrup. Serves 3.

Oven Pancake

1 cup milk
2/3 cup flour
2 tablespoons sugar

1/2 teaspoon salt
2 eggs
1/2 teaspoon ground cardamom
1/4 cup butter

Beat all ingredients, except butter, together until smooth. Place butter in a 9-inch pan and place in a 400° oven until the butter melts. Pour batter into butter and bake for 35 minutes or until deep brown and puffy. Serves 2.

Icelandic Pancakes

2 eggs
1/3 cup sugar
1/4 teaspoon salt
1/2 teaspoon cinnamon
1/2 teaspoon baking soda

1 teaspoon baking powder
1 1/2 cups flour
1/2 teaspoon vanilla
1/2 cup sour cream
2 cups milk

Beat all ingredients together until smooth. Batter should be thin. Pour a little batter on a hot griddle and spread it to form a thin layer across the bottom of the pan. When browned, flip and brown the other side. Repeat with remaining batter. Serve sprinkled with additional sugar. Serves 4.

Æbleskiver
Danish

8 eggs, separated
1 tablespoon sugar
2 cups flour, sifted

1 teaspoon cardamom
1/2 cup butter, melted
1 1/2 cups cream
butter

Beat together egg yolks and sugar. Add flour and cardamom; mix well. Add butter and cream; blend throughly. Beat egg whites until stiff. Fold into batter. Fry in *æbleskiver* pan*. Heat pan over medium heat, melt 1 teaspoon butter in each hole. Fill hole completely and bake for a few minutes. Turn and fry until golden brown. Serve hot with jam and sugar. Makes about 3 dozen.
*Found in specialty and culinary shops.

Norwegian Cream Pudding

2 cups whipping cream
1/2 cup flour
1 1/2 cups whole milk

1/2 teaspoon salt
2 tablespoons sugar
1 tablespoon cinnamon
1/2 cup sugar

Bring cream to a boil. Sift flour into cream while beating with a whisk. Beat until smooth. Cook 15 minutes or until mixture is thick and comes away from the sides of the pan. Continue cooking until butterfat separates from flour mixture; pour off butterfat and reserve. Slowly stir in the milk, salt, and 2 tablespoons sugar. Heat mixture to a boil. Beat with a whisk until smooth or if the lumps persist, pour mixture into a blender and blend until smooth. Combine cinnamon and remaining sugar. Serve pudding hot with reserved butterfat and cinnamon-sugar mixture. Serves 6 to 8.

Easy Rice Porridge

1 quart milk
1 cup rice
pinch of salt

1/4 cup sugar
stick of cinnamon
cinnamon and sugar
butter

Place milk, rice, salt, 1/4 cup sugar, and cinnamon stick in a pan and bring to a boil. Cover and place in an unheated oven for 6 to 8 hours. When ready to serve bring to a boil. Add additional milk if mixture is too thick. Serve hot with cinnamon, sugar, and butter. Serves 4 to 6.

Kringle from the O&H Danish Bakery

Racine, Wisconsin

For 2 Kringles:
3/4 cup butter, softened, divided
1 package or cake of yeast
1/4 cup warm water
1/4 cup lukewarm milk

1/4 cup sugar
1/2 teaspoon salt
1/2 teaspoon lemon extract
1 egg
2 cups sifted all-purpose flour

Butterscotch Filling:
1 cup brown sugar
1/3 cup butter

pinch of salt
pinch of cinnamon
1/2 egg white

Icing:
1 cup powdered sugar

water

94

(continued)

Kringle from the O&H Danish Bakery   *(continued)*

Kringle: Divide butter in half and spread each half on waxed paper to an 8x8-inch square. Chill. Dissolve yeast in warm water. Add lukewarm milk, sugar, salt, lemon extract, and egg, mixing well. Add flour and mix until smooth. Roll dough on well-floured board to an 8x12-inch rectangle. Place one piece of chilled butter on two-thirds of dough. Fold uncovered third of dough over the middle third, then fold the remaining third over the top. Again fold one end over middle third, and fold remaining third over top, making a square of nine layers. Wrap in waxed paper and refrigerate 30 minutes. Roll dough again to an 8x12-inch rectangle. Add second piece of chilled butter and fold the same way. This makes 18 layers. Refrigerate 2 hours. Cut dough into two equal pieces. Lightly roll one piece at a time, until piece is about 20x6 inches.

(continued)

Kringle from the O&H Danish Bakery *(continued)*

Filling: Mix filling ingredients until smooth. Spread center third of dough with butterscotch filling, then add fruit, nuts, raisins, and so on, or fill with jam. Fold one of the long edges to the middle, moisten other edge and fold over top to cover filling. Seal well. Put kringle on greased baking sheet and form into oval shape, pressing ends of kringle together to form a continuous circle. Flatten dough with hands. Cover kringle for one hour at 70°. Bake at 350° for 25 to 30 minutes or until golden brown. Cool.

Icing: Combine powdered sugar with enough water to form a thin glaze. Frost cooled kringle.

Note: Kringles keep very well in the freezer, or several days in the refrigerator. The high butter content keeps them moist.

Norwegian Pudding

Anita Hanson
Rapid City, South Dakota

Anita's husband is the pastor at Chapel in the Hills. The chapel is a replica of a twelfth century Norwegian church.

1/4 pound butter	1/2 teaspoon salt
3/4 cup flour	1 tablespoon sugar
1 quart whole milk, heated	butter
	sugar and cinnamon

Melt 1/4 pound butter and add flour; stir until smooth. Cook until bubbly. Gradually add milk, salt, and 1 tablespoon sugar. Cook until thickened. Serve with butter, sugar and cinnamon.

Christmas Rice Porridge

3/4 cup rice, uncooked
1/2 teaspoon salt
1 1/2 cups boiling water
2 cups whipping cream
2 cups milk
1 cinnamon stick
2 eggs, beaten

1 tablespoon butter
1/3 cup sugar
1/2 teaspoon ground cardamom seed
1 whole almond, shelled*
1/2 cup sugar
1 tablespoon ground cinnamon
2 cups 1/2-and-1/2 cream

Combine rice, salt, and boiling water. Simmer, covered, over low heat for 10 minutes. Add whipping cream, milk, cinnamon stick, eggs, butter, 1/3 cup sugar, cardamom, and almond. Place this mixture in a greased 2-quart casserole and bake for 2 hours at 325°. Combine remaining sugar and cinnamon. Serve rice pudding hot or cold with cinnamon-sugar mixture and 1/2-and-1/2. Serves 10.
*Whoever gets the almond gets to make a wish.

Skyr
Icelandic

4 quarts milk
1/2 cup milk
1 egg

1 tablespoon sugar
1/2 cup sour cream
12 drops rennet or 1/2 rennet pill
   dissolved in 1 tablespoon water

Scald 4 quarts of milk. Let cool to lukewarm or about 86°. Stir together the 1/2 cup milk, egg, sugar, and sour cream until smooth. Add rennet. Add to cooled milk and stir well. Set aside in a crock or bowl in a warm place, covered with a heavy towel or blanket, for about 24 hours. The milk should curdle. Strain whey from curds through a bag made of muslin or 3 thicknesses of cheesecloth. Stir curds well and serve with sugar and cream.

Fruit Pudding

4 cups fruit juice; a combination
   of orange, pineapple, and
   white grape is good
4 cups water
2 lemon slices

1 stick cinnamon
pinch of salt
sugar to taste
4 ounces (1/2 box) Minute Tapioca
1/2 cup white wine
whipped cream

Combine all ingredients except the wine and whipped cream. Cook over medium
heat until almost clear. Cool partially. Add wine and serve with whipped cream.

Kräm

Glen & Virginia Arnold
The Swedish Mill, Kingsburg, California

2 cups fruit juice
1 cup whole boysenberries
2 tablespoons cornstarch

3 tablespoons water
1/4 cup sugar
whipped cream

Bring juice and berries to a boil. Combine cornstarch and water. Stir sugar and cornstarch mixture into juice mixture. Cook until clear and thickened. Cool and serve with whipped cream.

Breads

Swedish Rye Bread

1 envelope active dry yeast	2 tablespoons sugar
1/2 cup warm water	2 tablespoons butter, melted
1 tablespoon fennel seeds	2 cups milk, scalded and cooled
1 tablespoon anise seeds	3 cups rye flour
1 teaspoon salt	3 to 3 1/2 cups all-purpose flour

Dissolve yeast in warm water; set aside 5 minutes. Crush fennel and anise seeds into a powder with a mortar and pestle. Add powdered seeds, salt, sugar, butter, milk, and rye flour to yeast mixture; beat well. Add enough flour to mixture to make a stiff dough. Let rest for 15 minutes. Turn dough onto a floured surface and knead until smooth, about 10 minutes. Wash bowl and grease. Place dough into bowl and turn once to grease top. Cover and let rise until doubled in bulk, about 2 hours. Punch dough down and divide into 4 parts. Shape each piece into a ball. Place the balls onto 2 greased baking sheets. Let rise for about 1 hour. Bake at 375° for 25 minutes, or until loaves test done. Cool on racks.

Finnish Rye Bread

1 envelope active dry yeast	2 teaspoons salt
1/2 cup warm water	1/4 cup butter
1 1/2 cups hot water	3 cups medium-rye flour
2 tablespoons honey	2 to 2 1/2 cups all-purpose flour
	melted butter

Dissolve yeast in 1/2 cup warm water. In a large bowl combine hot water, honey, salt, and butter. Cool to lukewarm. Add yeast mixture and rye flour. Beat with a wooden spoon until smooth. Work in enough all-purpose flour to make a soft dough. Knead until smooth and elastic, about 10 minutes. Wash and grease the bowl. Place dough in bowl and turn to grease top. Let rise until double in bulk, about 1 hour. Punch dough down and let rest 10 minutes. Form 2 loaves and place into well-greased 9x5-inch loaf pans. Cover and let rise until doubled. Bake at 400° for 30 minutes or until loaves test done. Brush tops with melted butter.

St. Lucia Saffron Rolls

Sweden

1 envelope active dry yeast
1/4 cup warm water
3/4 cup milk
1 teaspoon saffron threads or
    1/16 teaspoon powdered saffron
1/2 cup butter
1/2 cup sugar

2 teaspoons salt, divided
1/2 cup golden raisins
3 eggs, divided
3 1/2 to 4 cups all-purpose flour
2 tablespoons milk
1/4 cup sliced almonds
1/4 cup coarsely crushed sugar cubes
About 1/2 cup raisins for decoration

Dissolve yeast in warm water. In a saucepan, combine milk and saffron. Bring to a boil over medium heat, stirring until milk turns a deep yellow. Strain milk into a large bowl. Add butter, sugar, 1 teaspoon salt, and golden raisins.

(continued)

St. Lucia Saffron Rolls   *(continued)*

Cool and add yeast mixture and 2 slightly beaten eggs. Stir in enough flour to make a stiff dough. Turn out onto a lightly floured board and let rest for about 15 minutes. Wash and grease bowl. Knead dough until smooth, about 10 minutes. Return dough to bowl and turn to grease top. Cover and let rise in a warm place for 2 hours. Punch dough down and turn out onto a lightly oiled surface. Shape dough into a St. Lucia candle wreath or St. Lucia rolls. The candle wreath is created by dividing dough into 3 equal pieces. Roll each piece between your palms and on a lightly floured surface to make ropes 30 inches long. Braid ropes together. Cut off about 2 inches from each end of the braid and reserve. Place braid on a greased baking sheet and curve into a wreath. Pinch ends together. Shape reserved dough into a rope about 18 inches long and tie a bow, place the bow over the seam in the wreath. Let rise until doubled.

(continued)

St. Lucia Saffron Rolls   *(continued)*

To make St. Lucia rolls: Divide dough into 5 equal parts, then divide each of the 5 parts into 4 parts.   Roll each piece between your palms to form 6-inch ropes. Shape each piece into a letter S, coiling ends in spirals, as illustrated below. Lay 1 shaped rope across another, with center of top rope touching center of bottom rope. All spirals will curve in the same direction. Let rise until doubled. Beat together remaining egg, salt, and milk. Brush tops of raised dough with egg mixture. Sprinkle with sliced almonds and crushed sugar cubes. Bake at 375° for 20 to 25 minutes or until lightly browned. Cool on a rack. Decorate the bread with the raisins.

Shrove Tuesday Buns

1 envelope active dry yeast
1/4 cup warm water
2 eggs, divided
2/3 cup milk, scalded and cooled
1/4 cup sugar
1 1/2 teaspoons salt, divided
1/2 cup butter, softened

1/2 teaspoon ground cardamom or
   ground cinnamon
2 3/4 to 3 cups all-purpose flour, divided
2 tablespoons milk
8 ounces almond paste
1/2 cup whipping cream
2 tablespoons powdered sugar
additional powdered sugar

Sauce:
1/2 cup all-purpose flour
1/4 teaspoon salt
1/2 cup sugar

8 cups milk
4 teaspoons vanilla extract
2 tablespoons butter

(continued)

Shrove Tuesday Buns   *(continued)*

Dissolve yeast in water and set aside for 5 minutes. Beat in 1 egg, milk, sugar, 1/2 teaspoon salt, butter, spice, and 2 cups flour. Add enough remaining flour to make a stiff dough. Turn onto a lightly floured surface and knead for about 10 minutes. Wash and grease the bowl. Place dough into the bowl and turn once to grease top. Let rise until doubled in bulk, about 1 hour. Divide dough into 4, then divide each piece into 4. Shape each piece into a round bun about 1 inch high. Place on greased baking sheets; let rise for about 1 hour. Combine remaining egg, salt, and 2 tablespoons milk. Brush buns with egg mixture. Bake buns at 400° for about 10 to 12 minutes or until golden. Cool on racks. Cut almond paste into 16 slices. About 1/3 from the top, cut the buns horizontally almost through the bun. Insert a slice of almond paste into each bun. Combine the whipped cream and 2 tablespoons powdered sugar.

(continued)

Shrove Tuesday Buns   *(continued)*

Fill each bun with whipped cream until the top slice is held open by the whipped cream. Sprinkle powdered sugar over filling and bun.

Sauce: In a saucepan, combine flour, salt, and sugar. Slowly stir in milk. Bring to a boil over medium heat, stirring constantly. Cook until thickened. Stir in vanilla and butter until butter melts. Place hot sauce into 16 serving bowls and place a bun into the sauce.

Note: Unfilled buns may be frozen. To serve, thaw and fill.

Holiday Bread

2 envelopes active dry yeast
1/4 cup warm water
1/2 cup sugar, divided
2 cups milk, scalded and cooled
3 eggs, divided
1/2 cup butter, melted
3 teaspoons salt, divided
1 teaspoon crushed cardamom seeds
6 1/2 to 8 cups all-purpose flour

1 cup mixed diced candied fruit
1 cup golden raisins
1 cup slivered blanched almonds
2 tablespoons milk
1/4 cup coarsely crushed sugar cubes
1 cup powdered sugar
2 tablespoons water
1 teaspoon vegetable oil
1/2 teaspoon almond extract

Combine yeast, warm water, and 1 tablespoon granulated sugar; set aside for 5 minutes.

(continued)

Holiday Bread   *(continued)*

Stir in remaining sugar, milk, 2 slightly beaten eggs, butter, 2 teaspoons salt, cardamom, and 3 cups flour. Beat until smooth. Add enough of the remaining flour to make a stiff dough. Let rest for 10 minutes. Turn out onto a lightly floured surface and knead for 10 minutes. Knead in fruit. Wash and grease bowl. Place dough in bowl and turn once to grease top. Cover and let rise until doubled in bulk, about 1 1/2 hours. Divide dough into thirds. Shape each piece into a round loaf and place seam-side-down into 3 greased 8-inch round pans. Combine remaining egg, salt, and milk. Brush loaves with egg mixture. Let rise until doubled in bulk, about 1 hour. Brush loaves again with egg mixture and sprinkle with crushed sugar cubes. Bake at 375° for 25 to 30 minutes, or until loaves test done. Cool on racks. Combine powdered sugar, water, oil, and almond extract; spread over loaves.

Potato and Barley Flat Bread

1 cup buttermilk
1 cup mashed potatoes
1/2 cup melted butter
1 teaspoon salt

1 teaspoon baking soda
1 cup barley
2 cups uncooked rolled oats
2 cups all-purpose flour
melted butter for top

Combine all ingredients in order given. Stir to make a smooth dough. Turn out onto a barley-covered surface and divide dough into 4 parts. Roll out each part to make a circle of 10 to 12 inches in diameter. Place on greased baking sheets and pierce all over with a fork. Bake at 450° for 10 minutes. Brush with melted butter. Serve hot. Makes 4 loaves.

St. Urho's Day Rye Bread
Finnish

1 1/2 cups dark beer
1/2 cup milk
2 1/2 cups dark rye flour
1 cup cracked wheat
2 teaspoons salt
1 teaspoon crushed anise seeds

2 teaspoons crushed fennel seeds
1 tablespoon grated orange peel
2 envelopes active dry yeast
1/4 cup warm water
1 tablespoon dark corn syrup
2 to 2 1/2 cups bread flour

Heat beer and milk to a boil. Place rye and cracked wheat into a large bowl and add beer mixture. Add salt, anise, fennel, and orange peel. Let cool. Dissolve yeast in warm water; set aside for 5 minutes. Add yeast mixture and dark corn syrup to cooled mixture.

(continued)

St. Urho's Day Rye Bread   *(continued)*

Add enough bread flour to make a stiff dough. Let rest for 15 minutes. Turn onto a floured surface and knead for 10 minutes. Wash bowl and grease. Place dough in bowl and turn once to grease top. Cover and let rise until doubled in bulk, about 2 hours. Punch down and shape into a large loaf. Place loaf on a greased baking sheet. Let rise until doubled, about 45 to 60 minutes. With a sharp knife, slash top of loaf in 3 parallel cuts going each way to make 1-inch squares. Bake at 375° for 40 to 45 minutes or until loaf tests done.

White Potato Bread

1 envelope active dry yeast	3 eggs
1/2 cup warm water	1 cup cooked mashed potatoes
1/4 cup sugar	1 cup milk
1/2 cup butter, softened	6 to 7 cups all-purpose flour

Dissolve yeast in warm water; set aside for 5 minutes. Add sugar, butter, eggs, potatoes, and milk; beat until smooth. Gradually add enough flour to make a stiff dough. Turn onto a lightly floured surface and let rest for 10 minutes. Knead dough for about 10 minutes, adding flour as needed. Wash and grease bowl. Place dough in bowl and turn to grease top. Cover and let rise until doubled in bulk, about 2 hours. Punch dough down and divide in half. Shape each half into a loaf. Place in 2 9x5-inch greased loaf pans. Let rise until doubled in bulk, about 1 hour. Bake at 375° for 30 to 35 minutes, or until loaves test done. Cool on racks.

Cardamom Horns

1 envelope active dry yeast	2 eggs
4 tablespoons warm water	1 1/2 tablespoons salt
6 tablespoons butter	1 1/2 cups lukewarm milk
6 tablespoons sugar	1 teaspoon crushed cardamom seeds
	6 cups flour

Dissolve yeast in water; set aside for 5 minutes. Cream butter and sugar. Add yeast mixture and all remaining ingredients. Cover and let rise until doubled in bulk. Punch dough down and divide into 4 pieces. Roll out each piece into a circle and cut each circle into 8 wedges. Roll each wedge from the wide end and pinch end to seal, forming a horn. Place horns onto greased baking sheets and let rise until doubled in bulk. Bake at 375° for 10 to 12 minutes. Serve with butter.

Cardamom Crackers

These are made with a Norwegian "goro" iron, found in specialty shops.

3 eggs
1 cup sugar
1 cup whipping cream, whipped

1 cup butter, melted
1/4 teaspoon salt
1 teaspoon ground cardamom
6 cups all-purpose flour

Cut a pattern piece of paper the same size as the goro iron; set aside. Beat together all ingredients to make a stiff dough. Divide dough into 4. Roll out each piece to a rectangle that is about 1/8 inch thick. Cut dough using goro iron paper pattern. Place the iron on the stove over medium heat until a drop of water dropped on the iron sizzles and bounces off the iron. Place a piece of dough in the iron and close. Cook 1 to 2 minutes on each side, or until golden brown. Cool on rack. Repeat with remaining dough. Makes about 36 crackers.

Hard Tack

4 cups oatmeal

1 cup flour

1/2 teaspoon soda

1/2 cup sugar

1/2 cup butter, melted

1 cup milk

Combine all ingredients. Let stand overnight. Roll out dough very thin. You may have to use additional milk to get the dough to roll out. Cut into desired shapes and bake at 350° for about 10 to 15 minutes or until browned.

Cardamom Coffee Braid

2 envelopes active dry yeast	5 eggs, divided
1/2 cup warm water	8 to 9 cups all-purpose flour
2 cups milk, scalded and cooled	1/2 cup butter, melted
1 cup sugar	2 tablespoons milk
3 teaspoons salt, divided	1/2 cup sliced almonds
1 teaspoon freshly crushed cardamom	1/2 cup coarsely crushed sugar cubes

Dissolve yeast in warm water; set aside for 5 minutes. Stir in milk, sugar, 2 teaspoons salt, cardamom, 4 eggs, and 4 cups flour. Beat until smooth. Gradually add enough flour to make a stiff dough. Turn out onto a lightly floured surface; let rest for 15 minutes. Knead for 10 minutes.

(continued)

Cardamom Coffee Braid   *(continued)*

Wash and grease bowl. Return dough to bowl and turn once to grease top. Let rise until doubled in bulk, about 2 hours. Punch dough down and let rise again until doubled in bulk, about 45 minutes. Divide dough into 3; divide each piece into 3. Roll each piece between your palms to make rope 30 inches long. Braid 3 ropes together to make a loaf. Pinch ends together and tuck ends under loaf. Repeat with remaining dough. Place each loaf on a greased baking sheet. Let rise until doubled in bulk, about 45 to 60 minutes. Combine remaining egg, salt, and 2 tablespoons milk. Brush loaves with egg glaze. Sprinkle with almonds and crushed sugar cubes. Bake at 375° for 25 to 30 minutes or until crust is lightly browned. Cool on racks. Makes 3 braids.

Rusk

2 cups milk, scalded and cooled
2 envelopes active dry yeast
3/4 cup sugar, divided
7 to 8 cups flour

3/4 cup butter, melted
1 teaspoon salt
2 beaten eggs
1/2 teaspoon ground cardamom

Combine milk, yeast, and 1/4 cup sugar. Set aside 5 minutes. Add 1 cup flour, and 1/2 cup sugar. Set aside until bubbly. Add 4 cups flour, butter, salt, eggs, and cardamom. Gradually add enough flour to make a stiff dough. Turn out onto a lightly floured surface and knead for about 10 minutes. Wash and grease bowl. Place dough in bowl and turn to grease top. Let rise until doubled in bulk. Shape into 14 small loaves and place in small loaf pans. Bake at 350° for 40 minutes or until golden brown. Remove from oven and cool. On the following day slice and toast at 350° until browned.

Swedish Almond Rusk

1 cup sugar
1 cup oleo
2 eggs
3 tablespoons sour cream
1/8 teaspoon baking soda

3 cups flour
1 teaspoon baking powder
1 teaspoon almond extract
1/4 teaspoon salt
1/2 cup almonds, chopped

Cream sugar and oleo. Add eggs. Combine sour cream and baking soda; add to sugar mixture. Add remaining ingredients and mix well. Shape into loaves and place in 2 loaf pans. Bake at 350° for 30 to 35 minutes. When cool slice and toast.

Icelandic Brown Bread
Fred Bjornson, Cedar Rapids, Iowa

1/2 cup warm water
2 packages yeast
2 cups scalded milk
2 cups water
1 cup brown sugar

1/2 cup molasses
6 cups whole-wheat flour
4 cups white flour
1 teaspoon salt
1/2 cup melted butter

Dissolve yeast in warm water. Combine milk, water, sugar, and molasses. Cool to lukewarm. Add yeast mixture, salt, and 1/2 the flour. Beat until smooth. Gradually add the remaining flour and knead in the butter. Cover and let rise until doubled in bulk, about 1 hour. Punch down and let rise again for 1 hour. Punch down; knead. Divide into 3 or 4 loaves and place in loaf pans. Let rise again until doubled in size. Bake at 350° for 1 hour.

Cakes & Desserts

Easter Cheesecake
Finnish

1 gallon buttermilk
1 egg, beaten
1 cup sour cream
1/2 cup sugar
1/2 cup finely ground almonds

1/2 teaspoon vanilla extract
1/2 cup butter, melted
candied fruit
orange peel
whipped cream

Place buttermilk in a large casserole and bake at 250° for 3 hours. Cool. Line a sieve with cheesecloth and turn the buttermilk into the cheesecloth. Let drain overnight. Blend egg and buttermilk curd. Add sour cream, sugar, almonds, vanilla, and butter; blend well.

(continued)

Easter Cheesecake   *(continued)*

Place the mixture over medium heat, stirring constantly. Heat the mixture to 190° to 200°. Line a deep wooden *paskha* mold or a 1-quart clean crock with a double thickness of cheesecloth. Pour the mixture into the container. Place crock into a bowl. Place a weight on top of the container. Refrigerate 2 to 3 days. Excess liquid will seep into the bowl. To serve, unmold onto a plate and decorate with candied or fresh fruit and whipped cream. Serves 8 to 10.

Hanna's Apple Cake
Swedish

8 apples, thinly sliced
7 tablespoons butter
6 tablespoons sugar
3 to 4 bitter almonds, ground

3/4 cup ground blanched almonds
2 egg yolks
1/2 lemon, juice and grated rind
3 egg whites, stiffly beaten

Place well-drained apples into a greased baking dish. Cream butter and sugar until light. Gradually add all ground almonds, egg yolks, lemon rind, and juice. Fold egg whites into almond batter. Spread batter over apples. Bake at 400° for 15 minutes until golden.

Apple Cake
Danish

2 cups bread or cake crumbs	2 1/2 cups tart applesauce
3 tablespoons sugar, divided	1 cup whipping cream
1/2 cup butter	red jelly or jam for decoration

Brown crumbs with 1 tablespoon sugar in butter. In a 2-quart glass serving dish alternate layers of crumbs and applesauce. Chill. Whip cream with remaining sugar and cover cake with whipped cream. Decorate with jelly or jam.

Sandcake

1 1/2 sticks butter
3/4 cup sugar
3 eggs
2 cups flour

1 teaspoon baking powder
1/2 teaspoon vanilla
2 tablespoons milk
1 ounce sliced almonds

Line a loaf pan with greased waxed paper. Cream butter and sugar until light. Add eggs one at a time. Sift together flour and baking powder. Gradually add to butter mixture. Add vanilla and milk. Place mixture in a lined loaf pan and sprinkle with almonds. Bake at 350° for 1 1/4 hours, until firm to the touch. Remove from pan to cool. Frost if desired.

Norwegian Wedding Cake
Norma Wangsness, Decorah, Iowa

Norma is an artist. Her rosemaling is on the cover of this book.

3 cups butter, softened
1 1/2 cups almond paste
3 cups powdered sugar

3 teaspoons almond extract
6 egg yolks
7 1/2 cups sifted flour

Frosting:
1 1/2 cup sifted powdered sugar

1 egg white
1 teaspoon vinegar

Cream butter, almond paste, powdered sugar, and almond extract. Beat in egg yolks. Add flour gradually and mix until smooth.

(continued)

131

Norwegian Wedding Cake   *(continued)*

Place dough in a cookie press and press into *kransekake* ring molds, which can be purchased at specialty shops. If you do not want to invest in molds, shape the dough on foil-covered cardboard into 26 rings graduating in size. Start with a 1-inch ring and make each ring 1/2 inch larger than the one before. Bake at 350° for 15 minutes.

Frosting: Stir all ingredients together; add additional powdered sugar if the frosting is not stiff enough. Place in pastry tube with a small round tip.

To Assemble: Drizzle some frosting on a platter; this will anchor cake. Place the largest ring on the frosting. Apply frosting in scallops on the first ring and place the next largest ring on top of the first. Continue until you have used all 26 rings. The frosting will hold the rings in place. Decorate with small Norwegian flags or marzipan fruits on toothpicks.

Icelandic Prune Cake
Fred Bjornson, Cedar Rapids, Iowa

Fred was raised in Mountain, North Dakota, an Icelandic community.

1 cup butter
2 cups sugar
4 eggs
1/2 cup sour cream

1 teaspoon baking soda
1 teaspoon baking powder
5 to 6 cups flour
1 teaspoon cardamom

Filling:
3 pounds prunes

1 cup sugar
1 teaspoon cardamom
vanilla

(continued)

Icelandic Prune Cake   *(continued)*

Cream butter and sugar. Add eggs and sour cream. Sift together dry ingredients. Blend into butter mixture and knead slightly. Refrigerate for at least 1 hour. Divide dough into 10 parts. Roll dough out on a floured surface to fit 9-inch cake pans. Place dough in greased pans and bake at 350° for 10 minutes. Cool and stack like cookies.

Filling: Cook prunes until tender, reserve 1/2 cup of the cooking water. Pit and mash prunes. Combine reserved prune water, prunes, and sugar and cook until thick. Add cardamom and vanilla.

To Assemble: Place 2/3 cup of filling between each layer. Use 5 layers for each cake. Let stand for 24 hours before serving.

Lingonberry Torte

4 ounces unsweetened chocolate
1 cup milk
1 cup flour
1/2 teaspoon salt
2 1/2 teaspoons baking powder

4 eggs
1 egg yolk
1 1/2 cups sugar
2 teaspoons almond extract
lingonberry jam*

Combine chocolate and milk in the top of a double boiler. Cook over hot water until chocolate melts. Cool. Sift flour, salt, and baking powder together. Set aside. Beat together eggs, egg yolk, and sugar until light. Stir in almond extract, then the chocolate mixture. Fold in flour mixture; mix gently but thoroughly. Pour batter into 2 greased 9-inch cake pans and bake at 350° for 10 minutes. Reduce heat to 325° and bake 25 to 30 minutes longer, until the cakes test done. Cool several minutes, then invert on a rack and cool completely. Spread lingonberry jam between layers. Frost if desired.

*Lingonberry jam is found in Scandinavian import shops and museums.

Cloudberries & Whipped Cream

Morten Strand
Norsk Engros
Decorah, Iowa

A Norwegian favorite.

2 cups whipped cream

2 cups cloudberry preserves*

Fold the cloudberries into the whipped cream.

*Cloudberry preserves can be found in Scandinavian import shops.

Cookies & Candies

Icelandic Rolled Cookies
Fred Bjornson, Cedar Rapids, Iowa

2/3 cup sugar
1 cup butter, softened
1 1/4 to 2 cups flour, divided

1/2 teaspoon baking powder
1 egg yolk, beaten
sugar for sprinkling

Cream sugar and butter together. Combine 1 1/4 cups flour and baking powder; add to butter mixture. Mix well. Roll out on a floured surface and cut into desired shapes. Place cookies on a greased baking sheet. Brush with egg yolk and sprinkle with sugar. Bake at 350° for 10 to 12 minutes or until lightly browned.

Asa's Kleinur

Icelandic
Fred Bjornson, Cedar Rapids, Iowa

1 cup brown sugar
1 cup sugar
2 eggs, beaten
1 cup buttermilk
1/2 cup cream

2 teaspoons cardamom
1 teaspoon baking soda
2 teaspoon baking powder
1 teaspoon salt
5 to 6 cups flour, divided
oil for frying

Combine first 5 ingredients. Sift together cardamom, baking soda, baking powder, salt, and 5 cups flour. Add to buttermilk mixture with enough flour to make a soft dough. Turn onto a floured surface and roll out to 1/4 inch thick. Cut into 1x3-inch strips. Cut a slit into the center of each strip. Twist one end of the strip through the hole. Fry in oil like doughnuts until golden brown.

Berlinerkranser
Norwegian

1 cup powdered sugar
1 cup butter
2 eggs

3 cups flour
1 teaspoon baking powder
egg white
sugar for dipping

Cream sugar, butter, and eggs together. Sift together flour and baking powder. Add to sugar mixture; mix well. Roll pieces of dough into rope about the size of a pencil, about 4 inches long. Cross the ends and dip the top into the egg white and then the sugar. Place cookies on a greased baking sheet and bake at 375° for 8 to 12 minutes or until golden brown.

Wreaths

1 cup butter
3/4 cup sugar

1/2 cup cream
3 cups flour
sliced almonds

Cream butter and sugar. Add cream and flour; mix well. Refrigerate dough for about 1 hour. Roll out on a floured surface and cut cookies, using a doughnut cutter or 2 different-sized biscuit cutters. Place cookies on a greased baking sheet and sprinkle with almonds. Bake at 400° for about 8 to 10 minutes or until lightly browned.

Fruit Cookies

1 cup butter
1 1/2 cups sugar
2 eggs
2 1/4 cups flour, divided
1 teaspoon baking soda

1 teaspoon cinnamon
1/2 cup candied pineapple, chopped
1/2 cup candied cherries, chopped
2 pounds dates, halved
1 cup halved walnuts
1 cup whole filberts

Cream butter and sugar. Add eggs, 1/2 of the flour, baking soda, and cinnamon. Combine remaining flour and the dried fruits; toss to coat. Add fruit mixture and nuts to dough; mix well. Chill batter for about 1 hour. Drop spoonfuls of dough onto greased baking sheets. Bake at 350° for about 12 minutes.

Peppernuts
Danish

2 1/2 cups flour
1 teaspoon ground cardamom
1 teaspoon cinnamon
1/4 teaspoon white pepper

1 cup butter
1/2 cup sugar
2 eggs
grated rind of 1 lemon

Sift together flour, cardamom, cinnamon, and pepper. Cream butter and sugar; add eggs and lemon rind. Add dry mixture to butter mixture. Knead until a smooth dough is formed. Refrigerate 1 hour. Form small balls and place on a greased baking sheet. Bake at 325° for about 10 to 12 minutes or until golden brown.

Rosettes

3 eggs
1/3 cup sugar
1 cup flour

1/2 cup milk
1/4 teaspoon salt
oil for frying
powdered sugar for sprinkling

Beat eggs and sugar together. Add remaining ingredients. Beat until smooth. Heat a rosette iron in hot oil until hot. Dip iron in batter, making sure that the batter does not get over the top of the iron. Place iron into hot oil and cook rosette for about 1 minute; shake iron to remove the rosette. When rosette drops off remove it from oil and place on absorbent paper to drain. Sprinkle with powdered sugar.

Krumkage
Norwegian

1/2 cup butter
1/2 cup sugar
3 eggs

2 cups flour
1/2 cup cream
1 teaspoon vanilla

Cream butter and sugar. Add eggs; beat well. Add remaining ingredients and blend well. Heat *krumkage* iron* over stove. Place one teaspoon of batter in *krumkage* iron, close it and cook *krumkage* over medium heat on both sides. Remove from iron and shape into a cone, using a wooden spoon handle while still hot.
*Found in specialty shops.

Lutheran Lemon Bars
First Lutheran Church, Poulsbo, Washington

Lemon bars are a favorite of Lutheran church cooks for smorgasbords and suppers.

Crust:
1 cup butter, melted

2 cups flour
1/2 cup powdered sugar

Topping:
4 eggs

4 tablespoons lemon juice
2 cups sugar

Crust: Blend all crust ingredients together. Press into a 9x13-inch pan. Bake 20 minutes at 350°.

Topping: Beat together all ingredients. Pour over the baked crust. Continue to bake for an additional 30 minutes. Cool and cut into squares.

Finnish Christmas Prune Tarts

Pastry:
4 cups flour

1 pound butter, divided, softened
3/4 cup cold water

Filling:
1 pound pitted, stewed prunes

1/2 cup sugar

Pastry: Cut 1/2 butter into the flour until the mixture resembles corn meal. Add water. Chill 30 minutes. Roll out and dot with 1/4 pound butter. Fold dough from front to back, from back to front and from each side toward center. Chill. Repeat process of rolling and chilling, adding dots of butter 3 times or until all butter is used. Roll again. Cut into 3-inch squares. Slit each corner of each square.
Filling: Combine ingredients. Place a spoonful of prune filling in center of each square. Turn up alternating corners (as in making a pinwheel) and pinch together in the center. Chill. Bake at 400° for 13 to 15 minutes until golden. Cool.

Swedish Cookies

1 1/2 cups sugar
1 pound butter
3 egg yolks
4 1/2 cups flour

2 teaspoons baking powder
1 teaspoon almond extract
1 teaspoon vanilla
1/2 pound shelled pecans, halved

Cream butter and sugar. Add egg yolks and mix well. Add flour, baking powder, almond extract, and vanilla. Chill dough for about 1/2 hour. Roll dough into small balls and place on baking sheets. Press a pecan half into each ball. Bake at 400° for about 12 to 15 minutes.

Danish Butter Cookies

1 1/4 cups butter
1 1/2 cups sugar
3 egg yolks, unbeaten

2 1/4 cups sifted white flour
1 teaspoon baking soda
1 teaspoon cream of tartar
1 1/2 teaspoons almond flavoring

Cream butter and sugar. Beat egg yolks in, one at a time. Add remaining ingredients; mix well. Chill dough. Roll dough into small balls and place on an ungreased cookie sheet. Press dough with any press or glass dipped in sugar. Bake at 325° for 12 to 15 minutes. Remove immediately from cookie sheet and cool. Makes 2 1/2 dozen.

Spritz

1 1/2 cups butter
2 1/4 cups sugar
2 eggs, beaten

1 1/2 teaspoons vanilla
3 1/2 cups flour
1/2 cup finely chopped almonds
colored sugar for decorating

Cream butter and sugar. Add remaining ingredients and beat until smooth. Place dough in a cookie press and press out onto a greased baking sheet in the shape of small wreaths. Bake at 325° for about 10 minutes or until golden brown. Sprinkle with colored sugar. Makes approximately 150.

Almond Tarts

Pastry:
1 1/2 cups flour
1/2 teaspoon baking powder

1/4 teaspoon salt
1/2 cup butter
1 egg, beaten
1/3 cup sugar

Filling:
1/2 cup almond paste
2 eggs
1/2 cup sugar

1/3 cup butter, softened
1/2 teaspoon almond extract
1/4 cup milk

Topping:
1/2 cup powdered sugar

water
6 maraschino cherries

(continued)

Almond Tarts *(continued)*

Pastry: Sift together flour, baking powder, and salt. Cut butter into flour mixture until the mixture resembles corn meal. Beat egg and sugar together; add to flour mixture. Mix well. Place about a tablespoon of dough into 2-inch fluted pastry form and press so that bottom and sides are covered. Repeat with 11 more pastry forms.

Filling: Mix filling ingredients and beat until thick. Place about 1 1/2 tablespoons into each form. Bake at 375° for 30 minutes. Cool before removing from forms.

Topping: Mix powdered sugar with enough water to form a thin paste. Spread on tarts. Put 1/2 a cherry on top.

Marzipan Candy

1 pound almond paste
1 32-ounce jar marshmallow cream
1/3 cup light corn syrup

2 teaspoons vanilla
2 pounds powdered sugar
food coloring
plastic leaves

Cut almond paste into very small pieces. Add marshmallow cream and corn syrup; blend well. Add vanilla and enough powdered sugar to make the mixture easy to handle without sticking. Knead in the remaining powdered sugar one cup at a time. The dough with be stiff. Shape dough into small fruit shapes: apples, peaches, bananas, strawberries, etc. Let dry for at least 24 hours. Using a small brush paint with food coloring. Let dry on a wire rack for another 24 hours. Add plastic leaves to the appropriate fruit shapes.

Medals

Pastry:
1 1/2 sticks butter
2 cups flour

1/4 cup sugar
1/4 cup potato flour
1 egg yolk

Cream Filling:
2 eggs
2 tablespoons sugar

1/2 teaspoon vanilla
2 tablespoons flour
1 1/4 cups light cream

Icing:
1 tablespoon boiling water

1 cup powdered sugar
jam for decoration

(continued)

Pastry: Cut butter into flour until the mixture resembles corn meal. Stir in sugar and potato flour. Work in egg yolk until dough sticks together. Chill 2 hours. Roll out to 1/4 inch thick. Cut into 2-inch circles. Bake on greased baking sheets at 400° for 8 to 10 minutes. Cool on a rack.

Filling: Beat together eggs, sugar, vanilla, and flour. Bring cream to a boil. Slowly add to egg mixture. Return mixture to the saucepan. Cook stirring constantly until thickened. Cool completely.

Icing: Combine water and sugar. Take a cookie and spread with filling, top with another cookie and spread with icing. Decorate with a dab of jam. Makes 3 dozen.

Gingersnaps

2/3 cup butter
1 cup sugar
4 tablespoons sorghum
1 egg
1 cup flour

2 teaspoon baking soda
1/4 teaspoon salt
1/2 teaspoon ground cloves
1 teaspoon ground cinnamon
1 teaspoon ground ginger
sugar for rolling

Cream butter and sugar. Add sorghum and egg. Sift together dry ingredients; add to butter mixture. Chill at least 3 hours or overnight. Roll into 1-inch balls and then roll in sugar. Place on an ungreased cookie sheet. Bake at 375° about 10 to 12 minutes or until lightly browned. Makes about 2 dozen.

Note: Do not flatten the cookies. They will flatten in baking. Make a sample cookie first. If the top does not crack add more flour.

Fluted Cookie Tarts

1 cup butter
1 cup sugar
1 egg
1 teaspoon almond extract

3 cups flour
2 teaspoons lemon juice
1/4 cup chopped candied fruit
1 cup apricot preserves
1/4 cup toasted sliced almonds

Cream butter and sugar. Add egg and almond extract. Stir in flour; mix well. Place about 1 tablespoon of dough into 2 1/2-inch fluted pastry cups. Press dough to cover bottom and sides. Bake at 350° for 12 minutes or until light brown. Cool. Combine remaining ingredients except almonds. When the tart pastries are cooled, place a teaspoon of the filling mixture on each. Sprinkle with almonds. Makes 3 1/2 dozen.

May Day Crullers
Finland

1 envelope active dry yeast
2 tablespoons warm water
2 eggs
1 tablespoon sugar

1 cup milk, scalded and cooled
1/2 teaspoon salt
2 cups flour
oil for deep-frying
powdered sugar

Dissolve yeast in water and set aside for 5 minutes. Beat together sugar and eggs. Stir in yeast mixture, milk, and salt. Beat flour into mixture until smooth. Cover and let rise until bubbly, about 1 hour. Bring about 2 inches of oil to 375°. Pour 1 cup of batter into a pastry bag with a 1/4-inch tip. Squeeze batter through bag into hot oil, making swirling-circular designs, like bird nests. Fry 1 minute on each side or until golden brown. Remove to absorbent paper. Dust with sifted powdered sugar. Serve hot. Makes 15.

Finnish "S" Cookies

1/2 cup butter, softened	dash salt
1/4 cup sugar	1 1/2 to 2 cups flour
2 eggs, divided	sugar
1/2 teaspoon almond extract	1/4 cup finely chopped toasted almonds

Cream butter and sugar. Add 1 egg, almond extract, and salt. Mix well. Stir in enough flour to make a soft dough. Blend well. Roll pieces of dough between your palms to form long strands that are about 1/2 inch thick. Cut into 2 1/2-inch lengths. Beat remaining egg. Dip each 2 1/2-inch length into the beaten egg, then into sugar. Arrange in the form of an "S" on a greased baking sheet. Bake at 375° until golden, about 8 minutes. Cool on racks. Makes 3 1/2 dozen.